More Rubbish Pet Portraits

Hercule Van Wolfwinkle

Dedicated to the loving memory of Lisa.

Your love, enthusiasm and encouragement
will always be with me.

Foreword

Being honest, I was surprised when the good folks at HarperCollins wanted to make the first *Rubbish Pet Portraits* book with me, so I couldn't *believe* it when I found out they wanted to risk their careers again and make a follow-up!

For those unfamiliar with my work, I'm sorry for what you're about to see as you make your way through this book. For those who are familiar with my work, you deserve everything you get if you've decided to put yourself through this again.

All jokes aside, I was delighted to be able to make this second book of my 'rubbish' pet portraits, and that's only been possible because of your wonderful support, so thank you.

I draw my pet portraits for free. All I ask is that people make a donation to one of the charities I support if they are able to. Those charities are Turning Tides: Ending Local Homelessness and StreetVet, two amazing organisations that work tirelessly to help some of the most vulnerable in our communities.

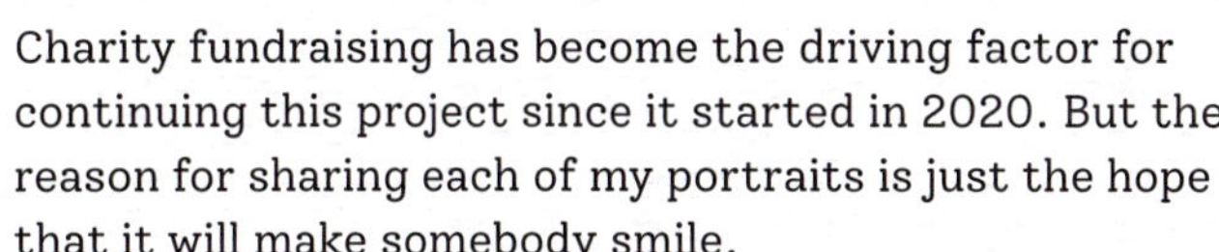

Charity fundraising has become the driving factor for continuing this project since it started in 2020. But the reason for sharing each of my portraits is just the hope that it will make somebody smile.

So, my hope is that this book is something you pick up when you need a little bit of silliness in your day. I hope it makes YOU smile, and I hope that you maybe share that smile with someone else who might need it.

Because the world needs more smiles and silliness like I need more art lessons!

Hercule Van Wolfwinkle

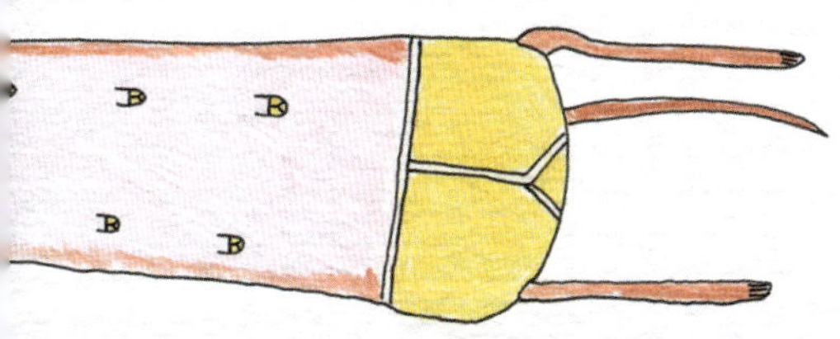

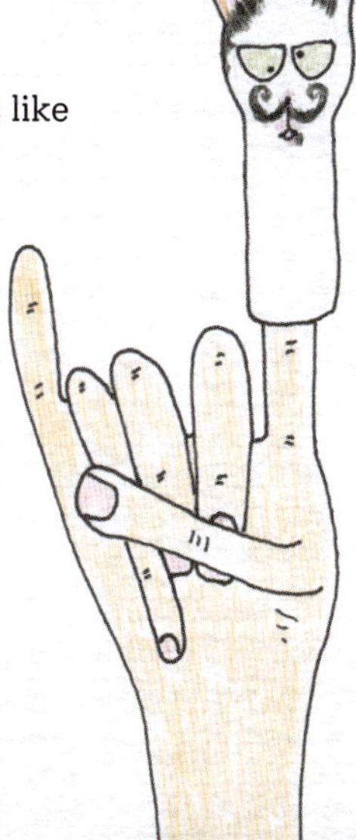

I've named this majestic beast **Brad Tits**.

I imagine Brad likes impressing guests with an impromptu offer of Viennetta and saying, 'Does that price include a coronation ceremony?' when the dentist tells him the price of his new crown.

Review from the customer:
'It reminds me of the time we got thrown out of a hotel in Cyprus because my grandad refused to wear a T-shirt in the restaurant despite numerous warnings and complaints.'

This is probably the biggest hamster I've ever seen in my whole entire life.

I don't know what he's called, but I've named him **John Gibraltar**.

Review from the customer:
'And if I show my brother
or even just my mother
You ain't stayin' alive,
stayin' alive . . .'

I've named this pair **Suzanne Barrell** and **George Balancing**.

Suzanne likes selling loose ends (some tied up) on eBay. George likes clenching his bum cheeks together to change pace on the dance floor.

Review from the customer:
'As you can see from the photograph, this pair fight like cat and . . . well . . . cat. But your portrait has united them in their hatred of it. It's the first thing they've agreed on in ages.'

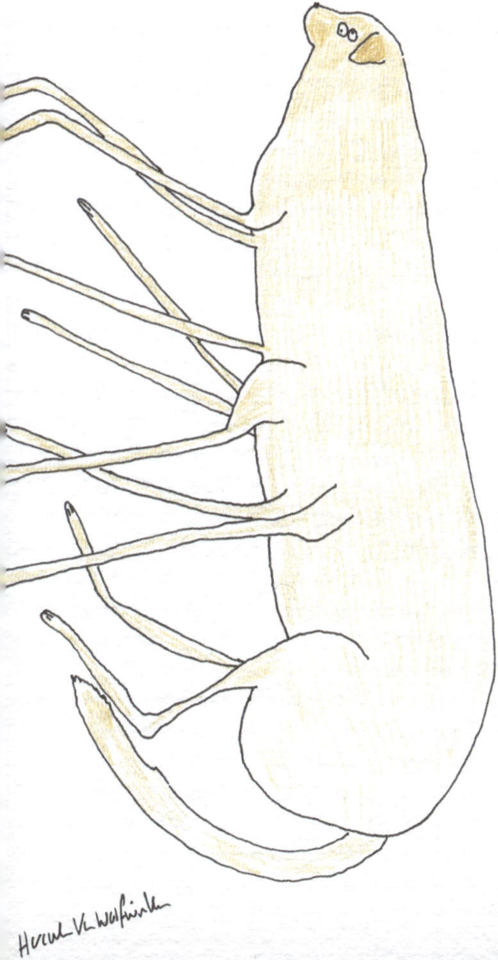

I've named this lazy bugger, **Dwayne 'The Socks' Johnson**.

Dwayne likes sustainably sourced belly rubs, urban morris dancing and telling anyone who'll listen about the Pontins hopscotch scandal of 1984.

Review from the customer:
'I've taken legal advice and, somewhat ironically, my solicitor said you haven't got a leg to stand on.'

They'll cross a poodle with anything nowadays, but I think crossing one with a giraffe is a little too much.

Debbie Llama, as I like to call her, likes landing herself in hot water with the local hot-tub salesman and saying, 'I don't like public displays of reflections,' when asked if she wants to go mirror shopping.

Review from the customer:
'I feel like a crime has been committed here. Shall I bag it for evidence?'

Show me a more realistic drawing of a chicken and I'll show you where you're wrong.

I don't know what he's called, but I've named him **Bob Dylhen**.

Review from the customer:
'How many wines must I sip
and down
Before I can call this a hen?

The answer my friend,
is it's going in the bin
The answer is it's going
in the bin.'

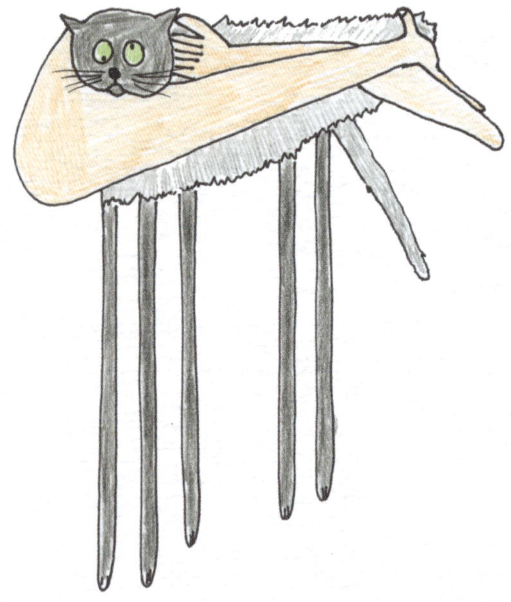

I don't know what this fuzzy feline is called, but I've named him **Keanu Squeeze.**

Keanu likes pin-striped underpants, saying, 'Table for two, please,' when getting on the bus and the thrill of being asked to play percussion during school assembly.

Review from the customer:
'They say accidents happen in slow motion, but this one looks like you've rushed it. With your eyes closed.'

I've named this young puppy **Justin Case**.

Justin likes taking gullible people for a ride on his e-scooter and the lonely (sometimes embarrassing) walk back from a buffet table.

Review from the customer:
'Normally it's artists who suffer for their work. With this project, you work and we suffer.'

I've named this handsome fella **Denzel Washwithtongue**.

Denzel likes long runs until the butcher gives up the chase, agreeing a safe word in the all-you-can-eat Chinese restaurant and selling anaesthetic to his local tree surgeon on Facebook Marketplace.

Review from the customer:
'I can actually put up with it . . . if I stand far enough back, squint a little and look at something else . . .'

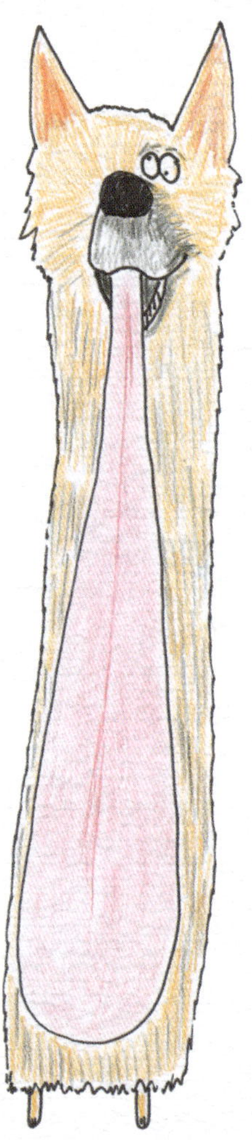

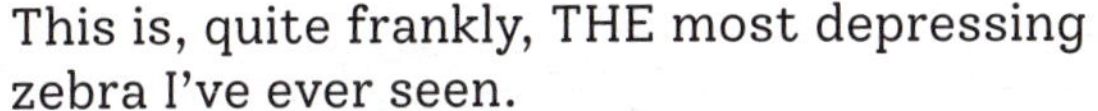

This is, quite frankly, THE most depressing zebra I've ever seen.

I imagine it must belong to a zoo, but the picture was submitted by the lovely Caroline Fussey.

I don't know what she's called, but I've named her **Catherine Zebra-Jones**.

Review from the customer:
'Call me fussy, but . . .'

Sorry, Caroline, I thought it was spelt 'Fussey'.

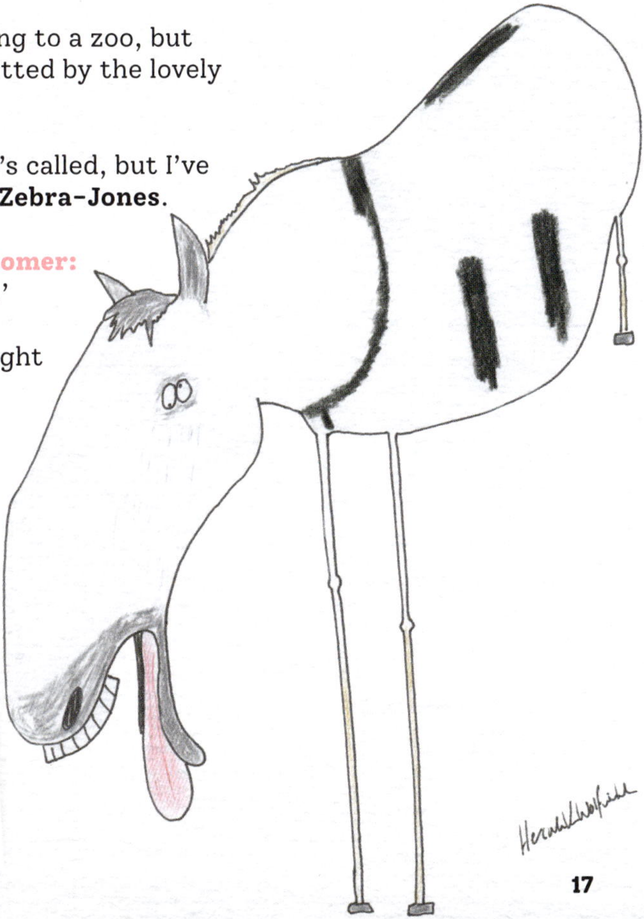

Cat? Exotic rabbit?
Long-haired guinea pig?
Wombat? Your guess
is as good as mine.

Review from the customer:
'Your art speaks to me . . .
It yells, "RUN, run for your
life and don't ever look
back . . . "'

I've named this little fella **Ross Unkempt**.

Ross likes amateur aerial photography, bootcut underpants and drunkenly eating macaroni cheese by fridge light.

Review from the customer:
'I was so close to having the perfect pet portrait. I mean, I hear the two people either side of you in the Yellow Pages are actually really good artists.'

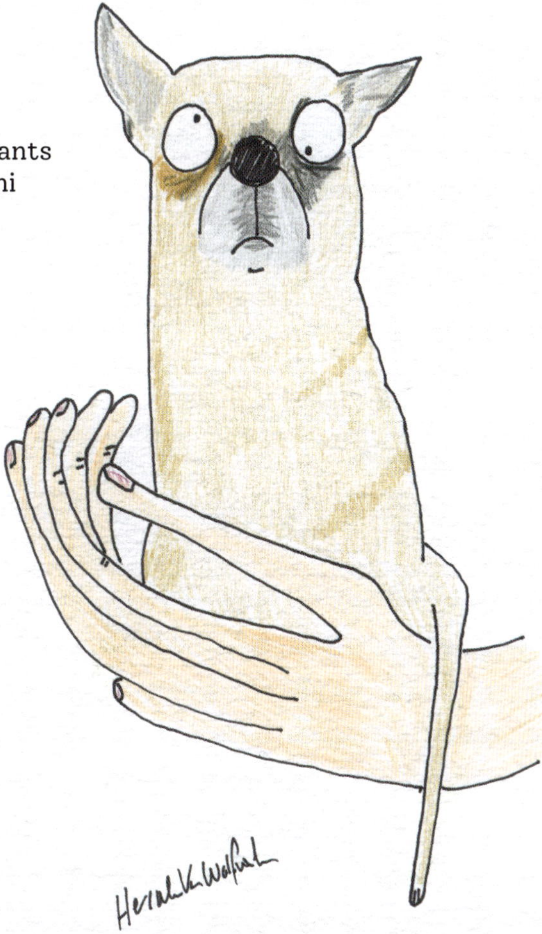

I've named this one **Elton Long**.

Elton likes the perceived authority of a laminated sign, lighting candles in awkward places and saying, 'It's been up and down,' when asked how his pogo-stick lessons are going.

Review from the customer:
'You probably want galleries to start recognising your work. I'd just like to recognise my dog . . .'

I've named this handsome stud **Al Pacinose**.

Al likes holding a grudge against the paperboy, complaining about hairs in his petrol down the BP garage and saying, 'We booked a sea view,' when getting on the bus.

Review from the customer:
'It looks like a cocktail sausage wearing a dunce's hat.'

This line-dancing pooch is called **John Sleaze**.

John likes feeling like a prude around dirty dishes, handing out compliments with reckless abandon and referring to his mother-in-law as 'The John Lewis Advert' because of her effortless way of making Christmas depressing.

Review from the customer:

'I genuinely reckon the dog could do a better self-portrait . . .'

This picture was submitted by the wonderful Jayne, who was lucky to see this wild Cornish badger on a recent visit to the West Country.

I've named her **Wendy Windsock**, Wendy likes dressing as a 1970s war correspondent, selling night-vision goggles outside Hollister and appearing to be well travelled on a first date by turning up with a box of Thorntons Continental.

Review from the customer:
'It's the best one by far. Far away. It's the best when you're far away. Far away from the picture. As far away as possible . . .'

I've named this bundle of joy **Scooby Don't**.

Scooby likes running till his bum whistles, purchasing more domain names than he needs and choosing tattoos from the Chinese take-away menu.

Review from the customer: 'I'm going to donate it to my local youth club. They were on the lookout for a new dart board and anti-climb paint. This will give them options for both.'

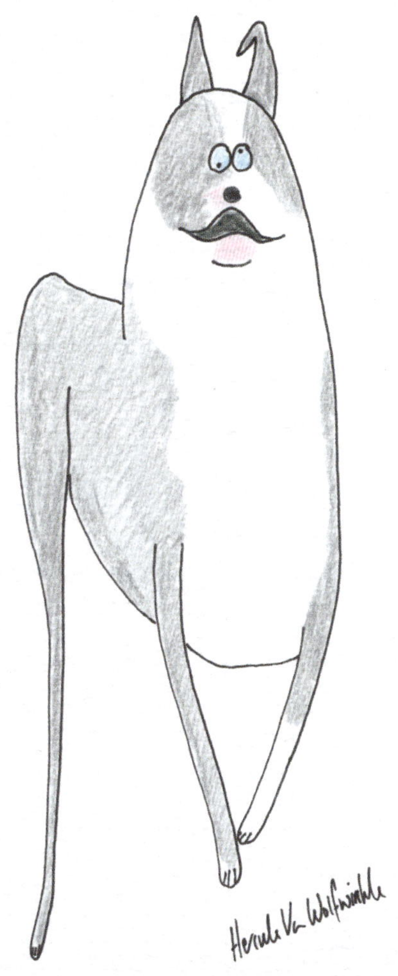

This chicken was photographed in the bath, but I wanted to draw it in all its beautiful glory so I used my artistic skill and animal knowledge to do a full-body portrait.

I don't know what she's called, but I've named her **Toyah Thrillcocks**.

Review from the customer:
'What came first, the chicken portrait or the eggs chucked at your house?'

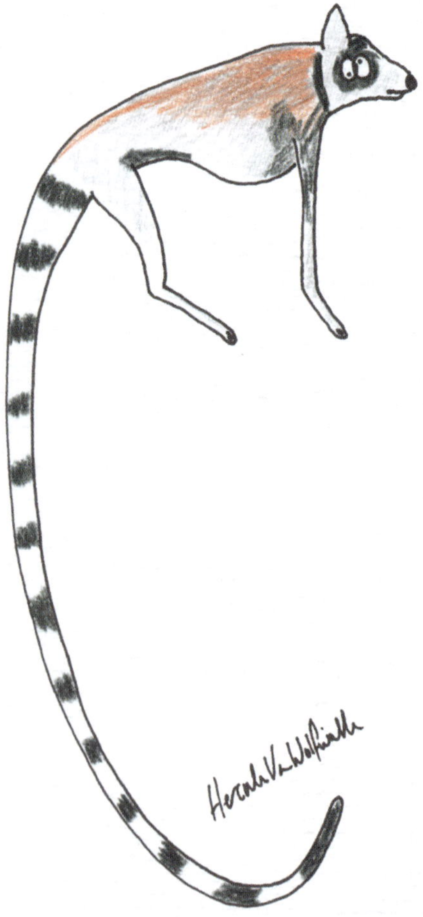

The wonderful Lucy messaged and said, ‘Please feel free to draw any animal in the picture . . .’

I don’t know what he’s called, but I’ve named him **Raymond le Mur** (that’s French for Raymond the Wall).

Review from the customer:
‘I suppose I should’ve known better. I’ll draw them myself.’

I've named this handsome fella **Linford Frisky**.

Linford likes running till he's out of sight, haunted houseplants and recreating *The Great British Bake Off* by inviting his elderly neighbour round to criticise his Victoria sponge.

Review from the customer:
'If I have one take-home from seeing your art, it's that I don't want to take any of it home.'

The owner of this dog asked if I could draw my portrait without the black bag. Of course I can, of course I can . . .

I don't know what the dog is called, but I've named her **Helen Stillin**.

Review from the customer:
'They say Every Little Helps, but my God, you need a LOT of help.'

I've named this one **Nicole Pigman**.

Nicole likes complaining to the vicar about her last cruise, selling pipe dreams to plumbers on the internet and flipping out when she's told her hour is up at the trampoline park.

Review from the customer:
'I ABSOLUTELY LOVE IT! Sorry, I suffer from premature appreciation; I hate it, absolutely hate it.'

I only like to draw the pets that appear in the reference photos, so I had a bit of a job removing the cage from this image; I think we'll all agree that I've nailed it, though.

Review from the customer:
'It looks like a dot-to-dot picture that's been drawn by someone who can't count. Or hold a pencil properly.'

I'll be honest, I've got NO IDEA what this is, but if I had to guess, I'd say some sort of exotic donkey.

I've named him **Peter Slouch**, and Peter likes doing, well, whatever the hell he likes because who's going to stop him?!

Review from the customer:
'I'll let my husband respond to you when he's back from his dog ride. I'm too angry to talk.'

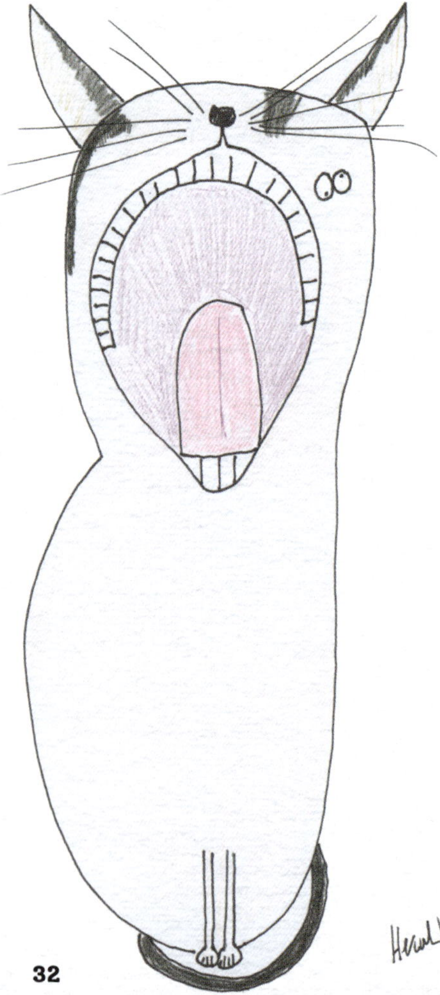

I've named this bored-looking feline **JK Yawning**.

JK likes second-hand corned beef, sitting on the fence when it comes to winding up the neighbour's dog and shouting from the rooftops about how much she misses her ladder.

Review from the customer:
'This portrait really channelled my inner magician; first I cut it in half and then I made it disappear . . .'

I've named this little Yorkshire terrier puppy **Michelle Phone**.

Michelle likes getting emotionally charged in a static caravan, adopting a cavalier attitude towards preheating an oven and injecting some excitement into a haircut with a well-timed sneeze.

Review from the customer:
'If I keep it for two years, can I then upgrade it for a better one?'

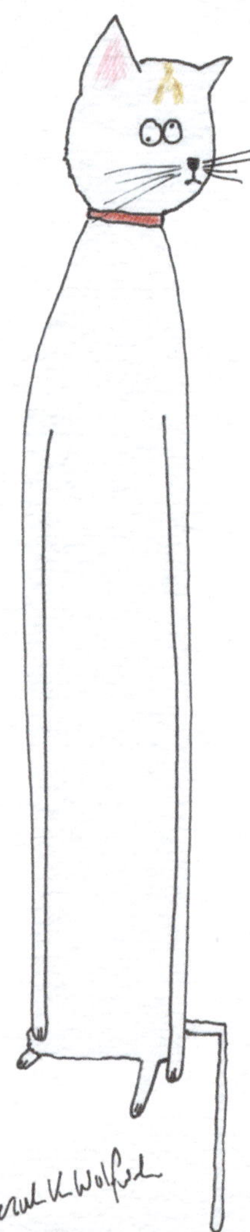

I've called this stand-up guy **Lance Armslong**.

Lance likes taking out his teeth for the big occasions, updating his cookie settings every time he goes to Greggs and feeling that lingering sense of pride that comes from hosting a successful buffet.

Review from the customer:
'Looking through your work is a real Tour de Farce.'

I've named this little beauty **Chaka Cant**.

It's a good job I had some landscape paper to hand for this one, as I usually only ever have portrait paper in stock.

Review from the customer:
'Does it come with a Certificate of Authenshiticy?'

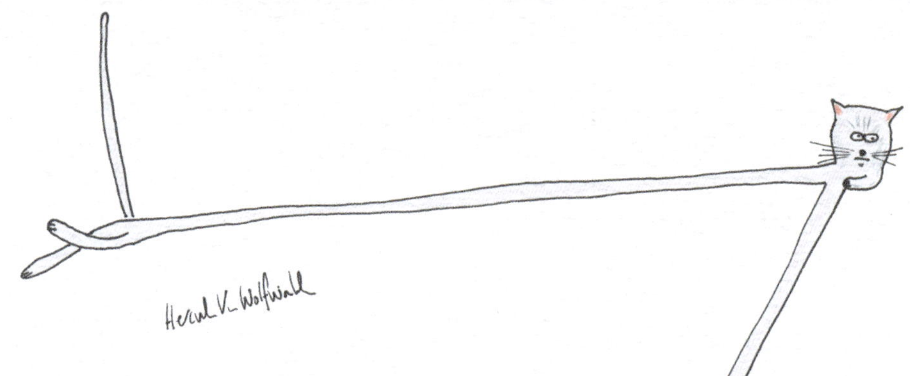

I've named this Dutch mountain ferret **Olivia Futon-Long**.

Olivia likes that slight sense of independence you feel when your hotel room has its own kettle.

Review from the customer:
'I can't find your complaints procedure. If there isn't anybody I can speak to about this, is there someone YOU can talk to? Preferably someone who can convince you to stop all of this nonsense?!'

This portrait was requested as a gift for the dog's dad, Burt. I've called the little scamp **Alan Slickman**.

Alan likes wading through puddles right up to his nipples and selling lithograph prints of bin-collection dates on Etsy.

Review from the customer:
'If I'm being positive, it's the second-best portrait I bought for Burt's birthday this year. If I'm being honest, I shouldn't have had to buy two.'

Because my portrait is all drawn in grey, I know you could be forgiven for thinking that it is just a photograph taken from the olden days. But it IS a drawing done in my ultra-realistic style.

Review from the customer:
'It looks like a skunk that's caught in an electric fence.'

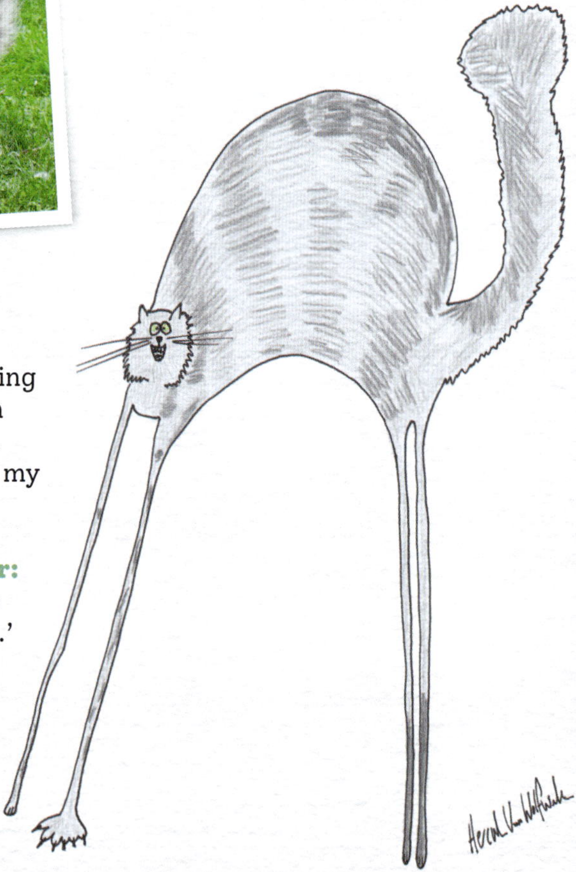

I've named this cool cat **Bryce Cube.**

Bryce likes calling shopkeepers 'boss', sneaking things into a skip and declaring that he's futon-intolerant when sofa shopping.

Review from the customer:
'Looks like a piece of toast that's been done on a broken grill.'

Meet **Barry Flier**.

Barry likes keeping a telephone line open at all times, side-stepping sawdust duty down the pub and saying, ‘I’ve brought my own stickers,’ upon arrival at the dentist’s.

Review from the customer: ‘It looks like a fried egg that’s hatched into a chicken.’

I've called this baggy pooch **Ray Shar Pei**.

Ray likes semi-detached caravans, winding up the foxes down the garage compound and holding a grudge against ice-cream vans who overcharge for a 99 Flake.

Review from the customer:
'I will treasure it. And by that, I mean I will bury it in a box on a deserted island to hopefully never be seen again.'

On the one hand this doesn't look like a boxer dog. But on the other . . . this athletic fella is **Floyd Whybother**.

Review from the customer:
'My advice to anyone thinking of getting one of these is: STOP, LOOK & LISTEN.

STOP before sending in your picture. LOOK at his other work (not for too long, though). LISTEN to all the other reviews.'

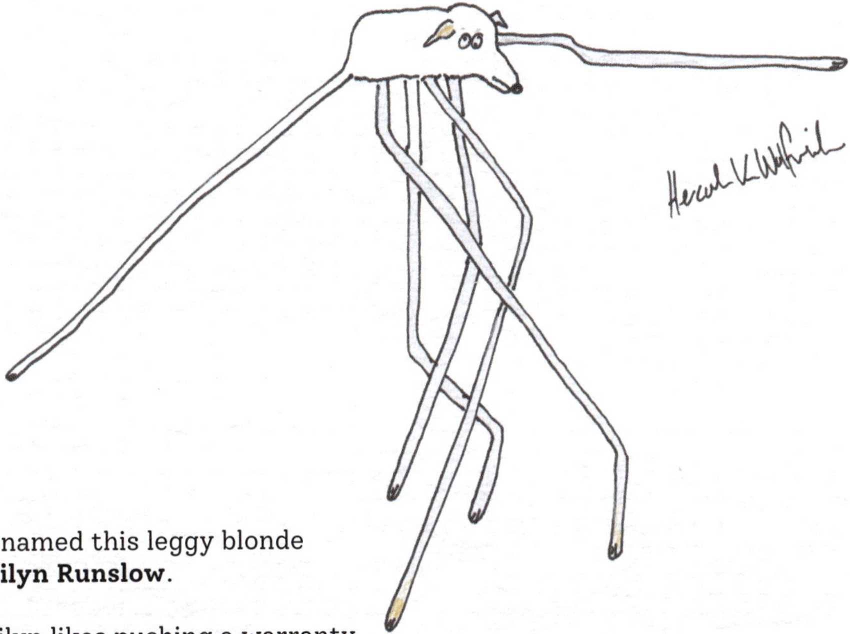

I've named this leggy blonde **Marilyn Runslow**.

Marilyn likes pushing a warranty to its absolute limits and coming to a mutual understanding with the roasting tin that it's as clean as it's ever going to get.

Review from the customer:
'There are some lessons to be learnt here. You need drawing lessons. I need to learn not to order pet portraits off the internet.'

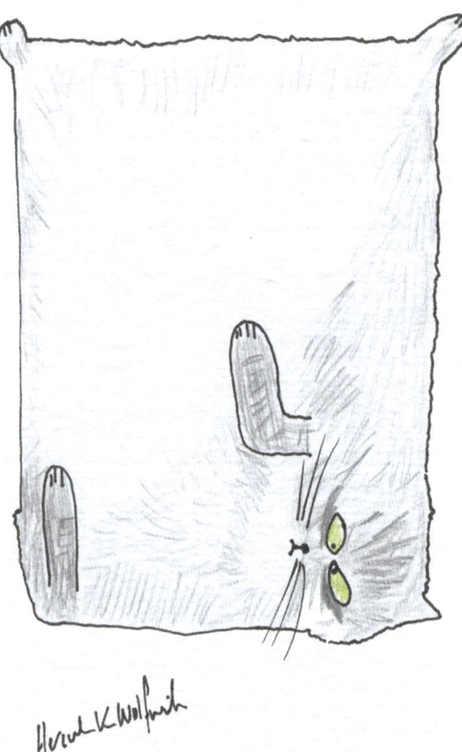

This . . . well, whatever it is, it belonged to the lovely Helen before being tragically hit by a steamroller (I assume that's what happened anyway).

Review from the customer:
'It reminds me of that time I saw a mouldy piece of bread getting chucked across a barber's floor . . .'

I've named this handsome chap **Jacob Sneak**.

Jacob likes moving his Nectar points to an off-shore account, gluten-free firelighters and saying 'Namaste' to the receptionist every time he leaves the leisure centre.

Review from the customer:
'It's a thing of . . . well, it's a thing.'

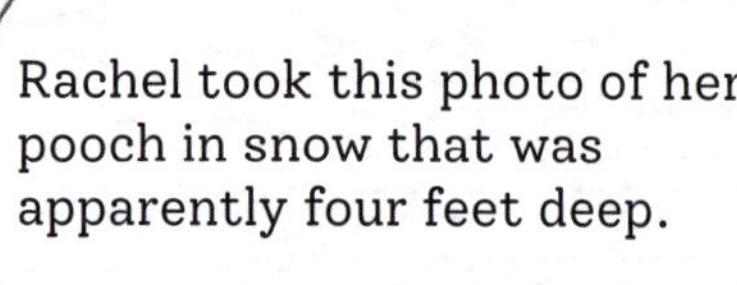

Rachel took this photo of her pooch in snow that was apparently four feet deep.

I don't know what he's called, but I've named him **John Backinsnow**.

John likes taking his own beer towel down the pub and saying, 'Pork balls, please,' like a tennis umpire when entering a Chinese restaurant.

Review from the customer:
'You want to charge me for THIS?! You cannot be serious . . .'

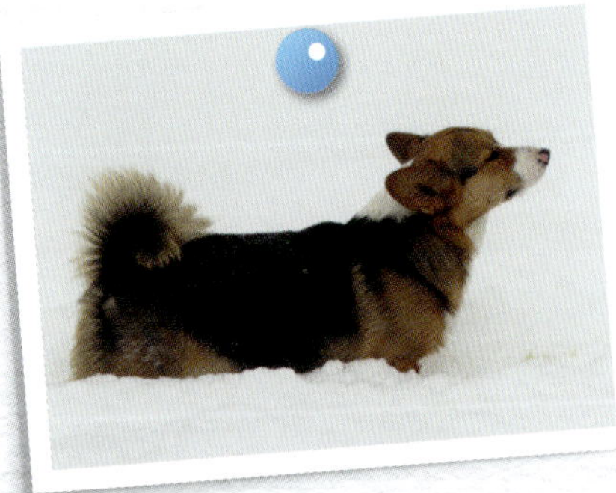

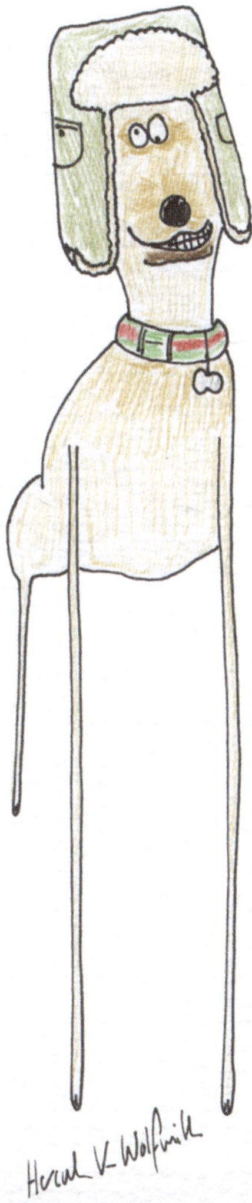

I've named this debonair dog **Georg von Trapperhat**.

Georg likes watching an argument brew out at sea, giving it everything he's got when squatting and saying, 'Can you just hold my plaice for a second?' when briefly leaving the queue at the fishmonger's.

Review from the customer: 'So long, farewell, the bins go out tonight . . .'

Being honest, this was an utterly terrifying portrait to tackle: a cat, feet AND two ghost pets all in one picture. But I think we can all agree that I've nailed it.

I don't know what the cat is called, but I've named him **Patrick Lazy**.

Review from the customer:
'Just when I think you can't possibly get better, you don't.'

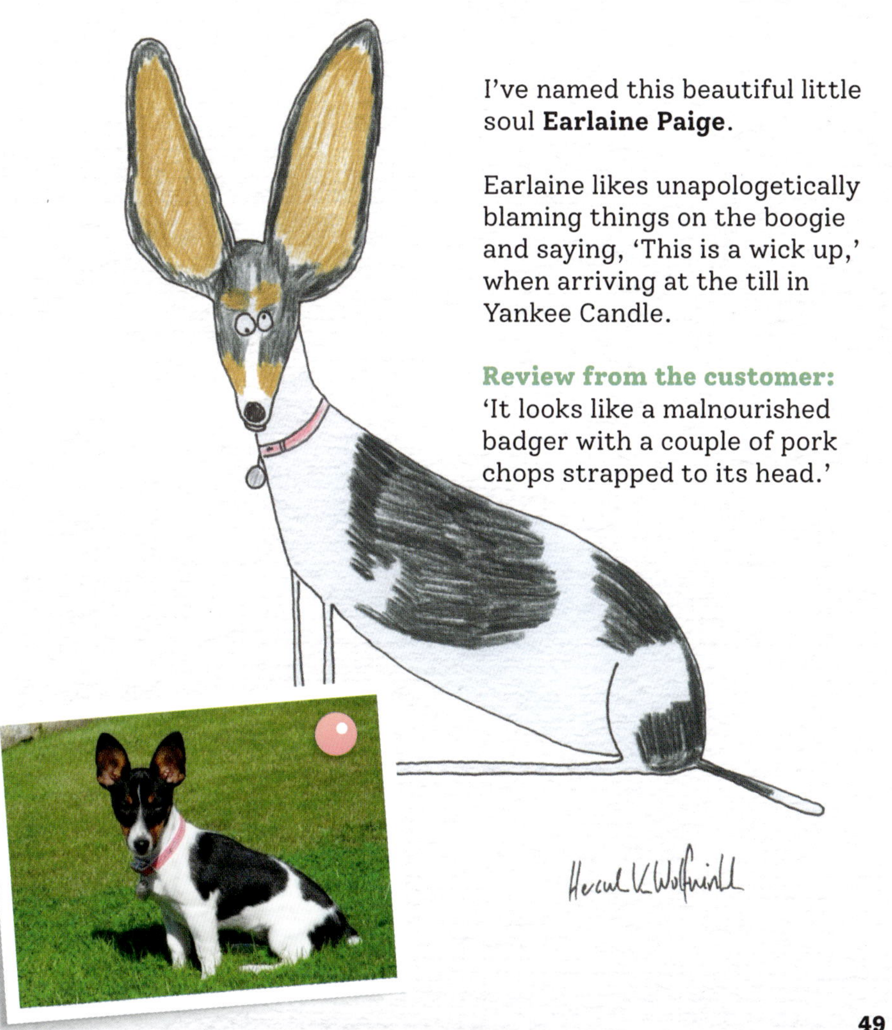

I've named this beautiful little soul **Earlaine Paige**.

Earlaine likes unapologetically blaming things on the boogie and saying, 'This is a wick up,' when arriving at the till in Yankee Candle.

Review from the customer:
'It looks like a malnourished badger with a couple of pork chops strapped to its head.'

I’ve called this old bird **Hen Stefani**.

Ms Stefani likes free-range cucumbers, checking her nasal hair for fleas and saying, ‘We’re just window shopping,’ when approached by a salesman at the conservatory showroom.

Review from the customer:
‘It’s like vegetarian meat replacement in portrait form; trying its very best to look like the real thing, but it’s disgustingly obvious that it isn’t.’

The dog here belongs to Alice and the guinea pig belongs to Connie.

I've named them **Liz Girlie** and **Liz Burly**.

Review from the customer:
'As the portrait features both our pets, we cut it in half. Then in half again. Then again. And again, until the bits were so small they could NEVER be put back together again . . .'

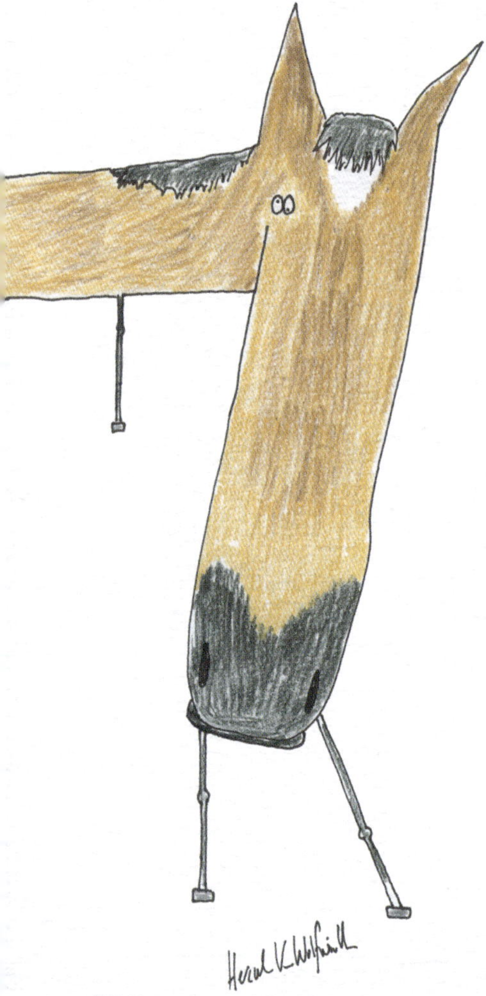

I've named this fine specimen **Gail Snorter**.

Gail likes a girl's night out down Ladbrokes, ugly crying to 80s ballads in the working men's club and having energy-efficient telephone calls with the mother-in-law.

Review from the customer:
'Did you draw it through a letterbox while looking at the original photograph against the frosted glass?'

I'm sure some people just sometimes send me pictures of 'stuff', not pets. I've named this one **Stirling Mops**.

Stirling likes long walks on the extendable handle and doing blow-offs that sound like a distant frog croaking in the bulrushes.

Review from the customer:
'The envelope read "DO NOT BEND". It would've shown more care if it had read "DO NOT SEND".'

I've named this handsome chap
Robbie Sillyarms.

Review from the customer:
'Your pen has gone and done it here
I think you need a new career
Shake my fist, my kids in tears
I screamed
It's now a burning effigy
The worst thing I will ever see
I wish you had some empathy, my dear

So come on, let me . . . complain to you.'

This fine stallion is known as **Dwight Mare**.

Dwight likes regrouting his false teeth, showing off his apps down the gym, and the thrill and excitement of a deleted WhatsApp message in the group chat.

Review from the customer:
'I'm wondering if this can be blown up? Not in size, into smithereens . . .'

Answers on a postcard, please, if you have any idea what this is. I don't have a clue, but I've named it **Charles de Hairball**.

Review from the customer: 'At first I thought I must have sent you the wrong picture by mistake, because I do have a photograph of a mouldy plum on my camera from a recent Tesco complaint . . .'

I've named this little beauty **Kat Mandon't**.

Kat likes handwash with extra helpings of sea kelp, smoking vapes that smell like success and 'Bring your own problems to work' day.

Review from the customer:
'It's the worst thing I've ever had on my wall. And my friend's kid once launched a full nappy across my lounge . . .'

I’ve named this handsome fella **Tongue Hardy**.

Mr Hardy likes recycled embarrassment, shadows from the olden days and haggling over the price of stepladders at car boot sales to make his real ladder jealous.

Review from the customer:
‘You shouldn’t have. No, really, you really shouldn’t have . . .’

This ravishing rodent is **Alicia Cheese**.

Alicia likes authentic Scottish hummus, getting too big for her boots when shopping for wellies and telling her new guitar tutor that their teaching methods really strike a chord.

Review from the customer:
'I can't even begin to tell you how much I like it. Because I don't like it. I hate it.'

I've named this little fella **Brad Splits**.

Brad likes selling rumours about estate agents, saying, 'Please mind the gap,' when visiting the dentist and wondering if you can only milk almonds when they're pregnant.

Review from the customer:
'Art should evoke emotion. Well, this gives me similar emotions to that time the local youths spraypainted "art" all over the garage compound.'

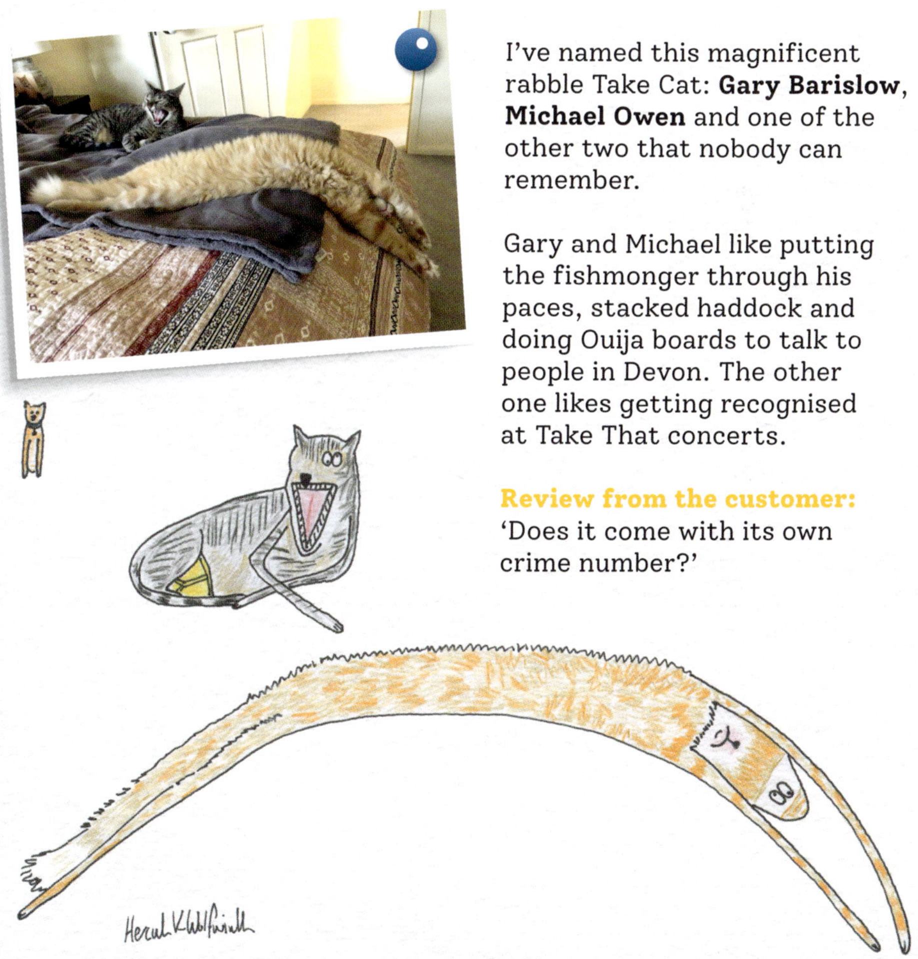

I've named this magnificent rabble Take Cat: **Gary Barislow**, **Michael Owen** and one of the other two that nobody can remember.

Gary and Michael like putting the fishmonger through his paces, stacked haddock and doing Ouija boards to talk to people in Devon. The other one likes getting recognised at Take That concerts.

Review from the customer:
'Does it come with its own crime number?'

This parrot portrait is titled **'Stevie Blunder'**.

Review from the customer:
'Isn't she lovely? No.
Isn't she wonderful? Also no.
Isn't she precious? See previous answers.'

Meet **Janice Popped-in**.

Janice likes being wary of men with long toes, updating her password at the speakeasy and self-shame by fridge light on Sundays.

Review from the customer:
'I always try to move on from disappointments as fast as I can. In fact, I now hold the record for the fastest 100 metres travelled with a wheelie bin.'

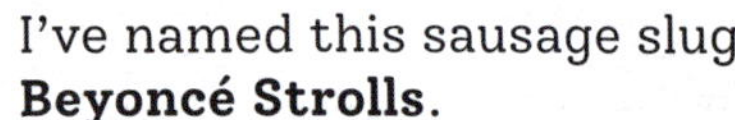

I've named this sausage slug **Beyoncé Strolls**.

Beyoncé likes impressing guests with a well-timed offer of a choc ice, not being one of the 99 problems and complaining about the quality of the inflatable pillows under her airplane seat.

Review from the customer:
'My brain has told my eyes that they've just lost their no-claims discount.'

This fine beast is **Babe Hoof**.

Babe likes reheated sushi and campaigning for his local council to declare the pothole on his street a nature reserve, as it got so big it developed its own ecosystem.

Review from the customer:

'I nearly fell out of my chair when I saw this for the second time. The first time I saw it, I needed to sit down.'

A word of warning, folks. Don't let Lucy's dog in your gran's lounge when the budgie is flying about.

I don't know what this pair are called, but I've named them **Stacey Collagen** and **Joe Squashed**.

Review from the customer:
'You're an absolute natural. A natural disaster.'

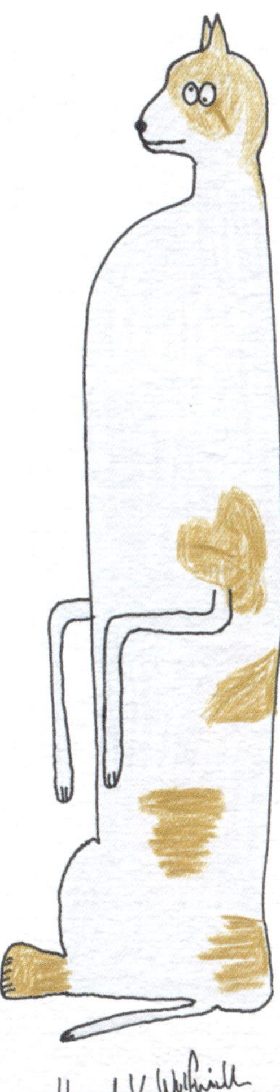

This curious little fella is **Vincent Stand-off**.

Review from the customer: 'They say that sometimes an artist needs to take a break from a piece they're working on . . .

Can I suggest that you take a break from this one and then get back to it when you've actually learnt how to draw?'

I've named this piece **Justin Shot**.

Justin likes pretending he's Mary Berry when heating up Homebake Petit Pains, getting backhanded compliments from his tennis coach and ensuring that he carries a cup of coffee with him AT ALL TIMES.

Review from the customer:
'It reminds me of something.
Obviously not my dog, but something . . .
. . . a hamster peeping out of a baguette, maybe . . .'

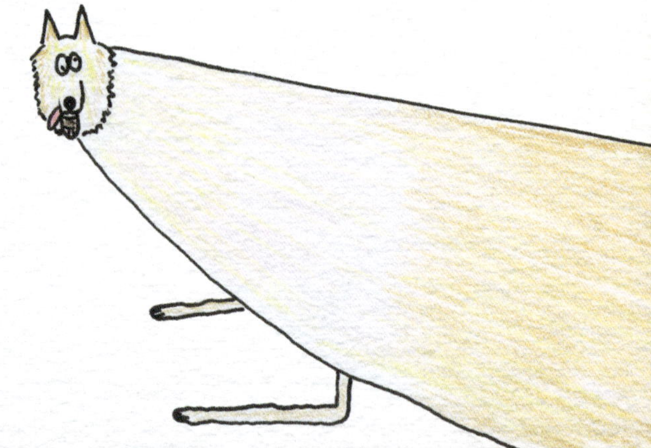

This furry loaf is **David Hasacough**.

David likes haddock who take cod's name in vain, whistling the *Top Gun* theme tune during foreplay and doing blow-offs that sound like a damp Yellow Pages landing on a doormat from a height.

Review from the customer:
'Some pictures hang in the darkness, afraid to be viewed in the light . . .'

This abandoned scarf has been named **Lee Thargic**.

Review from the customer:
'I've moved it to an offshore account.

I say "offshore", but I really mean I flushed it down the bog . . .'

I've named this baby horse **Ray Ricotta**.

Ray likes deodorant that smells like a campsite toilet block, undermining confident fathers in front of their kids and showing off his Duke of Edinburgh Award to passing ramblers.

Review from the customer:
'It looks like a potato that's going to a fancy-dress party as Michael Fabricant.'

I know he's got his eyes closed in the reference photo, but I've drawn this wire-haired Yorkshire terrier with his eyes open because it's rude to watch animals when they're sleeping.

Review from the customer:
'Your portrait is bullying my eyes.'

The wonderful Claire took this great picture of a horse from three-quarters of a mile away.

I don't know what he's called, but I've named him **Brian Noculars**.

Review from the customer:
'This is the worst thing that's happened to me since my horse took out a restraining order and I wasn't allowed within 400 feet of him.'

Hercule K Wolfgrind

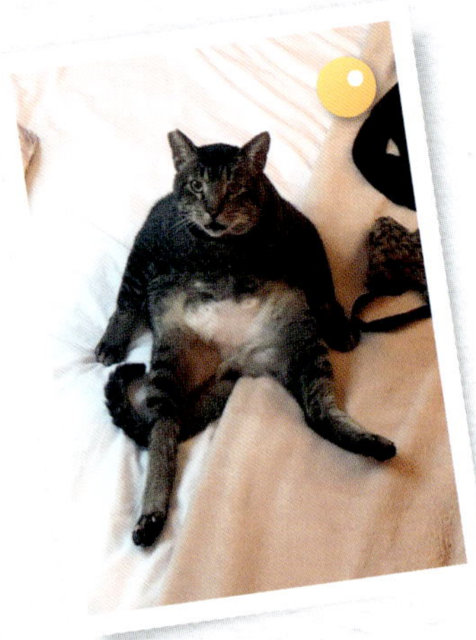

This fine specimen of the feline form is **Donald Slump**.

Donald likes being reckless with his five-a-day and getting in a muddle with 'In case of emergency break glass' instructions.

Review from the customer:
'Sadly, the cat is no longer with us. He's still alive – we just had to get rid of him because he kept reminding us of your awful portrait.'

I've called this little chonk **Paul Nutwhip**.

Paul likes flirting with the novelty doorstops down Dunelm Mill, ordering mixed Italian herbs on every food shop (just in case) and plumping up cushions with extra helpings of ice cream.

Review from the customer:
'You've made him look like a certain well-used emoji. Which is probably fitting, because that's exactly what your portrait is . . .'

This pretty little thing is **Patti O'Doors**.

Patti likes sneaking up on her cholesterol levels and asking the butcher if their 'minted lamb' makes all its money in a Ponzi scheme.

Review from the customer:
'If talent runs in your family, I can only assume you have a very large clan and you were at the end of the queue . . .'

This pygmy wolf is **Simon Howl**.

Simon likes unsmoked mackerel with extra nicotine patches, impressing first dates with his National Record of Achievement Book and pre-arranged fights with Attila the Swan by the village pond.

Review from the customer:
'Well, at least I now know what Hugh Jackman would look like if he had an allergic reaction to chewing on a horseshoe . . .'

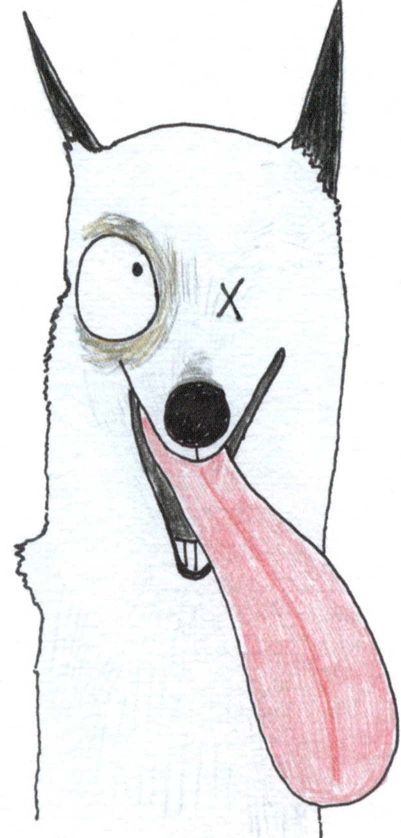

This one-eyed bandit is **Squint Eastwood**.

Mr Eastwood likes seeing a job halfway to completion, impatiently leaning over toddlers in the Toby Carvery queue and keeping presumed-dead cacti on the kitchen windowsill ‘just in case’.

Review from the customer:
‘If good things come to those who wait, I don’t mind waiting a little longer . . .’

I've named this beautiful pooch **Husky Springfield**.

Ms Springfield likes dry-scone stalling down the garden centre café, saying, 'Do we bring our own creosote?' when booking fencing lessons at Center Parcs and doing blow-offs that sound like a snowman falling over in the dead of night.

Review from the customer:
'I grew a beard that looks more like my dog than your portrait does . . .'

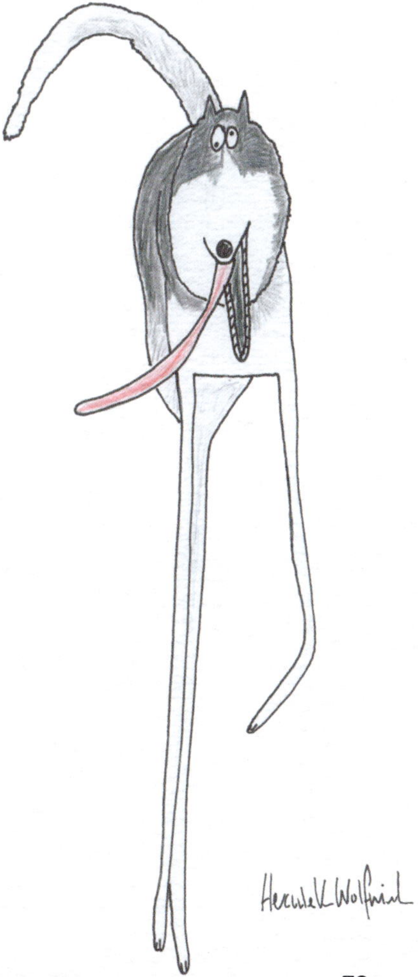

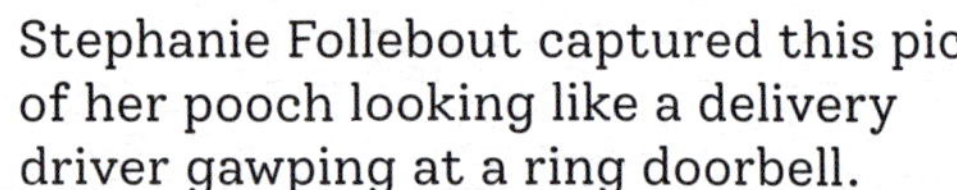

Stephanie Follebout captured this pic of her pooch looking like a delivery driver gawping at a ring doorbell.

I don't know what he's called, but I've named him **Slobbing Hood**.

Review from the customer:
'You really are making contributions to the art world. Granted, it's akin to Godzilla's contribution to city planning, but it's a contribution nonetheless . . .'

I thought you only saw wild guinea pigs in Papua New Guinea, but Ayeshea was lucky enough to get a photo of this one on a mountain in Norfolk.

I've named him **Hairy Styles**.

Review from the customer:
'"You've captured it perfectly" is exactly what I would say if you were drawing Gandalf after an industrial accident at the Wotsits factory . . .'

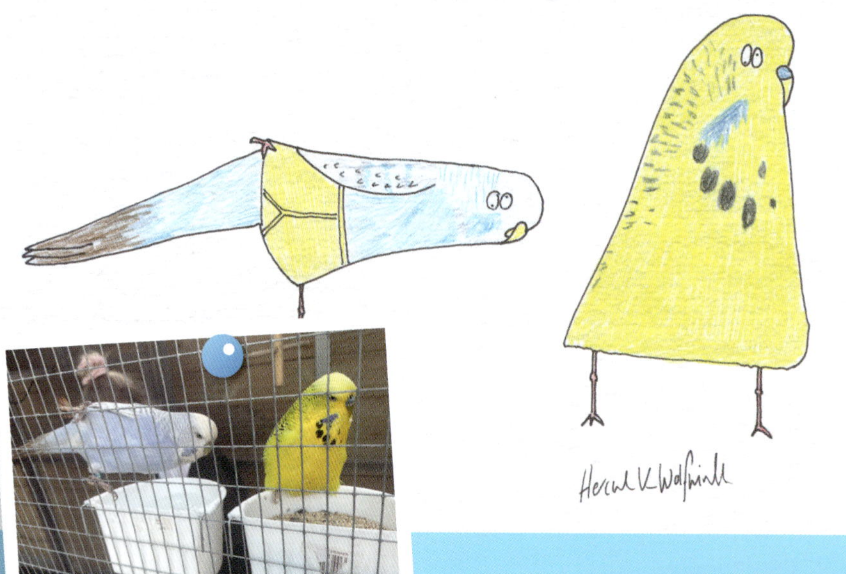

This pair belong to the amazingly wonderful Elsa Cooper.

I don't know what they're called, but I've named them **Chesney Squawks** and **Stephen Squawking**. Stephen likes motivating lazy garlic, getting into public spats with the editor of a small-town magazine and taking his sock puppets to entertain the vicar in the confessional booth.

Chesney secretly likes Stephen, but he hides it by rugby-tackling him in public.

Review from the customer:
'I'm going to give it to my dad to look after. Because Mum says he's always losing things . . .'

This giant Amazonian horsefly was photographed by the wonderful Arwen.

I've named him **Jeff Coldbum**.

Jeff likes flirting with windows, making false claims about his toilet habits, and judging the quality and price of a jam by nothing other than its packaging.

Review from the customer:
'As an artist myself, I'd love to give you some pointers . . . preferably with a big stick.'

I've named this mysterious creature **Tim Peek**.

Tim likes mock-Tudor underpants, 'Take your own anxiety to work' day and replying with a simple (yet ambiguous) 'loads' when asked if he wants sugar in his tea.

Review from the customer:
'I spy with my little eye, something beginning with "crap". If you want a clue, it ends in "pet portrait" . . .'

This absolute unit is **Orson Swells**.

Orson likes surprising the dentist with some well-placed sweetcorn, sticking with his bag for life for the sake of the kids and replying, ‘Only if it’s got tuna in it,’ when asked by a waiter if he’d like some water for the table.

Review from the customer:
‘It looks like a neglected boiled egg . . .’

I've named this handsome chap **Bruce Trellis**.

Bruce likes recreating the thrill and excitement of camping by putting his duvet in the freezer an hour before bedtime and inviting the neighbours round to hear him fart in the night.

Review from the customer:

'I'd like to thank you so much. This has cured my extreme fear of being burgled; now I'm almost wishing for it . . .'

This long-legged guinea pig is **Alfred Nickssocks**.

Alfred likes canned laughter in brine, keeping an excuse with him at all times and taming wild rocket in the salad drawer.

Review from the customer:
'Maybe it's time to take up a new hobby? I hear paper shredding and pencil snapping are quite enjoyable pastimes . . .'

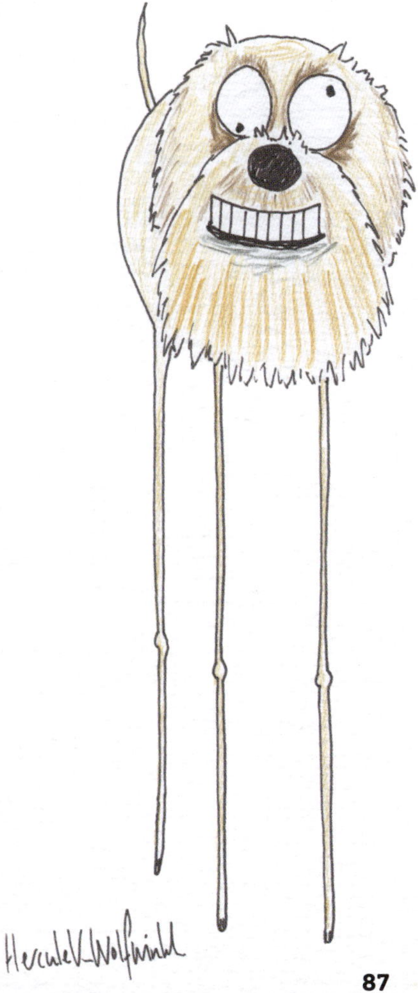

I don't know what this chicken is called, but I've named him **Rafa Beneatheggs**.

Rafa likes stopping for a half-time orange while on hold to his energy provider and taking his own ambience with him to the Toby Carvery.

Review from the customer:
'Sometimes you have to stand back to really appreciate art. I had to stand in a different postcode to appreciate this piece.'

Don't you hate it when you're taking a photo of your nice new carpet tiles and the dog gets in the way? Well, that's exactly what happened to Ian recently.

I don't know what the pooch is called, but I've named him **Myles Away**.

Review from the customer:
'At least you've left enough blank page for me to write down all the things I hate about the portrait . . . well, half the things at least . . .'

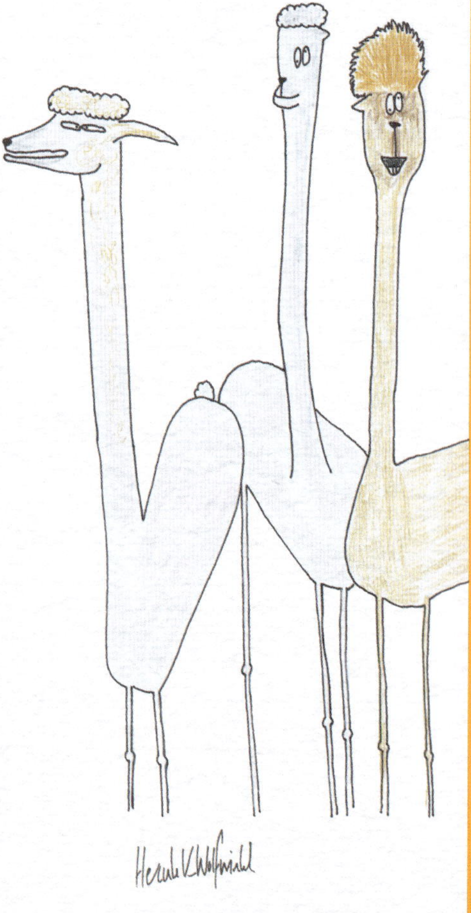

How many times in life do you get to draw one camel, nevermind three?!

I've named this lot **Llama Del Rey**, **Adam Thellama** and **Brad Spits**.

Review from the customer:
'My eyes have filed for divorce.'

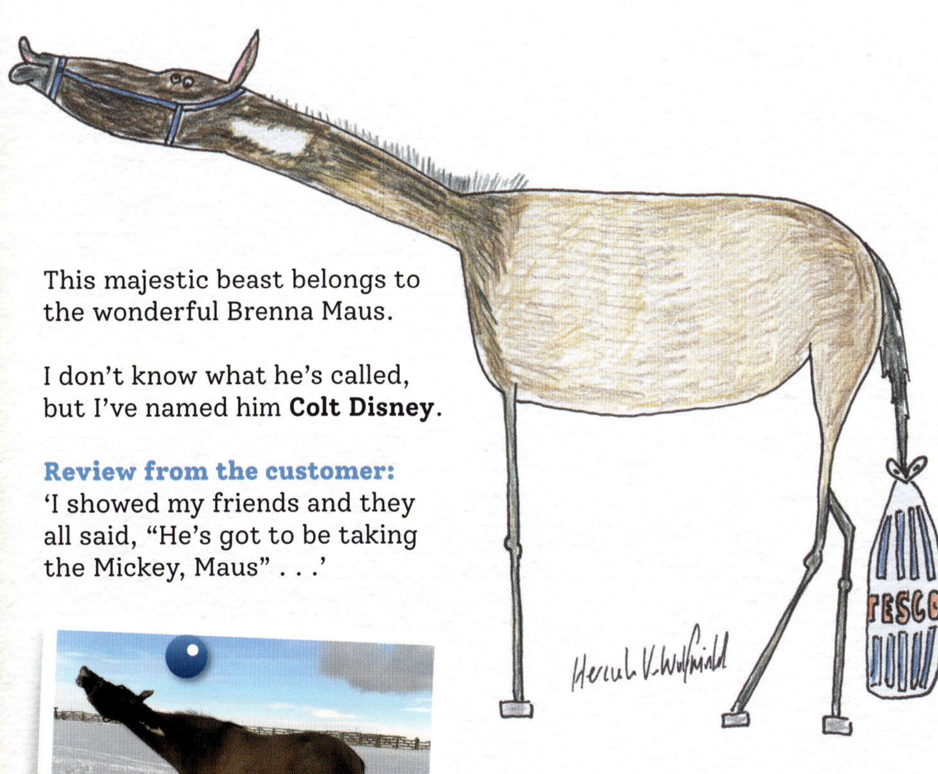

This majestic beast belongs to the wonderful Brenna Maus.

I don't know what he's called, but I've named him **Colt Disney**.

Review from the customer:
'I showed my friends and they all said, "He's got to be taking the Mickey, Maus" . . .'

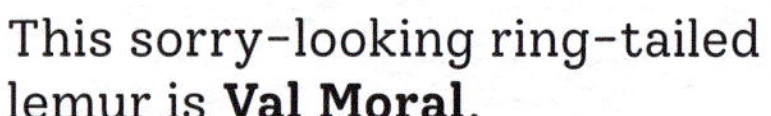

This sorry-looking ring-tailed lemur is **Val Moral**.

Val likes practising her butterfly stroke at the botanical gardens and injecting some excitement into jury service with a well-timed Mexican wave.

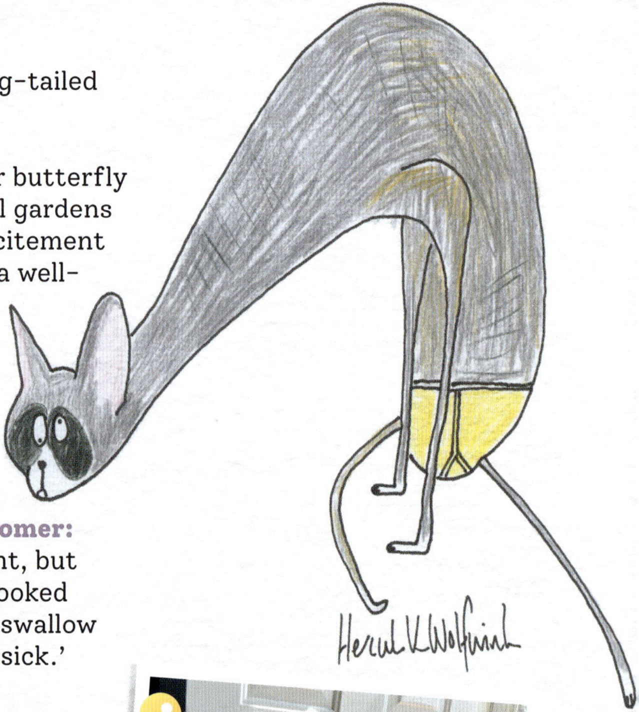

Review from the customer:
'I've heard of raw talent, but your art is like undercooked meat: rushed, hard to swallow and leaves you feeling sick.'

The wonderful Jessica was lucky enough to get a picture of this chicken mid-hatch.

I don't know what he's called, but I've named him **Orson Shells**.

Review from the customer:

'My tortoise is going to live for another 100 years and I can safely say that this is the worst thing that's ever going to happen to him . . .' (Not sure why you showed my chicken portrait to your tortoise, Jessica, but OK.)

This is, without a shadow of a doubt, the biggest gerbil I have EVER seen!

I've named her **Lynn Chilla**.

Lynn likes chicken-free chickpeas and saying, 'Is this form designed to test your patients?' when filling out questionnaires at the doctor's.

Review from the customer:
'It looks like Mr Blobby after a particularly messy divorce . . .'

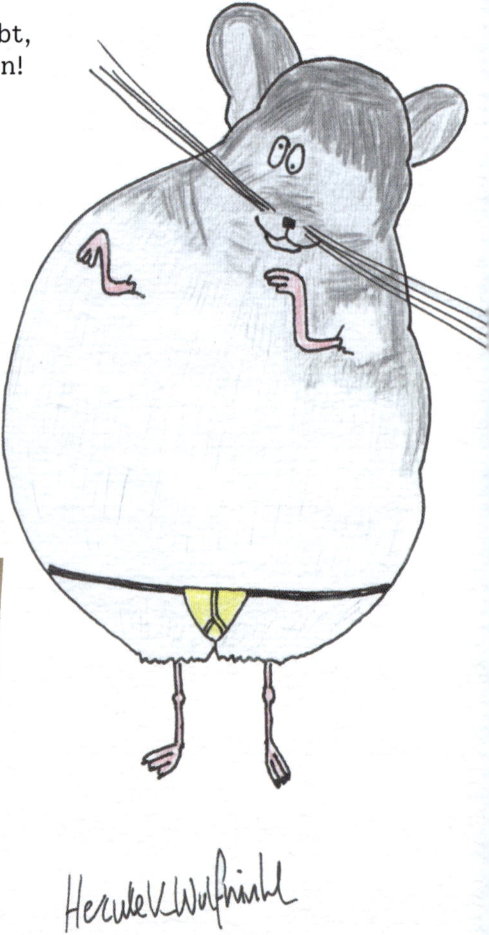

Nathaniel sent in this picture of his pooch and, if you look closely, you can just about make out an image of the infamous 'ghost dog' that haunts the A17 just outside of King's Lynn!

I don't know what the dog is called, but I've named him **Mo Farahnormal-Activity**.

Mo likes running around in circles until his privates twist together and saying, 'Where can I set up my pottery wheel?' when arriving at speed-dating night down the community centre.

Review from the customer:
'It's like an endurance test for my eyes and emotions!'

I've named this detached beard **Mick Dungarees**.

Mick likes hanging around the laundrette on payday, extra-large chips with a splash of self-loathing and saying, 'Worst bingo ever!' when the dentist starts shouting numbers at their assistant.

Review from the customer:
'I reported you to Trading Standards, who said they'd look into it. They later replied to say that they never want to look at anything else you've drawn again.'

This is a surprisingly short-haired version of the long-haired Hungarian guinea pig.

I don't know what he's called, but I've named him **Martin Swoons**.

Martin likes windswept-look hair gel, the ease with which Battenberg cake can be ignored and giving whey to bodybuilders round the back of the leisure centre.

Review from the customer:
'This is a case of Pen Behaving Badly . . .'

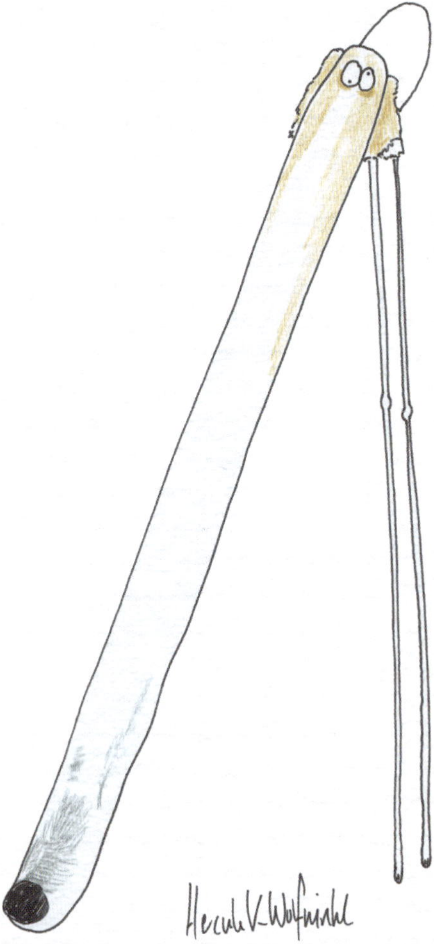

I don't know if anteaters are really classed as pets, but I've named this one **Yoko Grownose**.

Yoko was once banned from her local artisan café for eating an entire bowl of minestrone soup with the 'table number' wooden spoon.

Review from the customer:
'They say that sometimes things have to be at their worst before they get better. And judging by this, you're about to get better . . .'

I've named this distinguished fellow **Bill Toupee**.

Bill likes saying, 'May I approach the bench?' whenever he arrives at a bus stop and asking the Starbucks barista for legal advice to get off a shoplifting charge.

Review from the customer:
'The only person who should be judging your work is the sort who sits at the front of a courtroom.'

I don't know what this cheeky cat is called, but I've named her **Mariah Carefree**.

Review from the customer:
'I sent you a picture of my beautiful cat and you've sent back a drawing of what appears to be a mouse eating its way out of a mouldy satsuma.'

I call this one **Yasser Hadahat**.

Yasser likes streaking on a work Zoom call, impersonating the kitchen bin when plates are being scraped and confessing to the priest that he finds it hard to whisper.

Review from the customer:
'Weirdly, we're no longer in a party mood . . .'

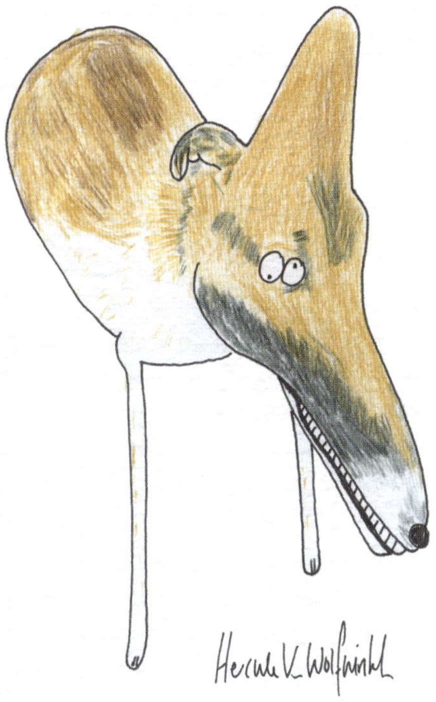

I've called this nosy parker **Meryl Peeps**.

I've obviously had to use all my animal knowledge and artistic skill to recreate this portrait and show her in all of her glory.

Meryl likes selling left-handed ironing boards round the back of Argos and impressing guests with the speed at which she can defrost frozen profiteroles.

Review from the customer:
'I wanted my dog portrayed, not betrayed . . .'

I've named this crowd of mischief-makers **Dave, Roger**, **Syd**, **Rick** and **Nick**.

Stink Floyd (as they're collectively known) like yelling, 'Worst conga EVER!' when trying to get some excitement into the post-office queue.

Review from the customer:
'I don't even know where to begin with this. And neither did you by the looks of things . . .'

This pretty little lady is **Beatrice O'Dent**.

Trix likes yelling, 'Jams ahoy!' whenever she turns into the preserves aisle of Tesco.

Review from the customer: 'I don't know if it was lost in translation, but when I said I wanted one of your portraits "real bad", this isn't exactly what I meant . . .'

I've called this one **Fleur Ball** and, whatever it is, it haunts the home of the lovely Becky.

Fleur likes selling nicknames to gang members round the back of the garage compound and lobbying her local MP for a more visible optician presence on the high street.

Review from the customer:
'I know you don't charge for these, but I really want to give you something for it . . . a punch on the nose!'

This handsome fella is **Lee Raffe**.

Lee likes referring to his local 'pick your own' farm as 'the vegan safari park', taking his own judging panel to the National Fencing Championships and singing, 'Nope, shoulders, knees and toes, knees and toes . . .'

Review from the customer:
'You've got some neck trying to charge me for this . . .'

This pair of low-slung hounds are **Chintz Charles** and **Camilla Barks-and-Groans**.

Charles likes saying, 'Time for the enthronement ceremony,' whenever he does a smelly blow-off.

Camilla likes Charles because he once told her he had loads of Nectar points.

Review from the customer:
'Talking of disappointing sausages, I must respond to Ken and Barbara at No. 33 and tell them I can't attend their BBQ this weekend . . .'

This grumpy little bugger is called **Lookatma Shandy**.

Lookatma likes referring to house plants as 'delayed disappointment', doing blow-offs that sound like a duck mimicking an ice-cream van and attempting to beat the Guinness World Record for the most amount of disappointment served in one trifle.

Review from the customer:
'Just when I thought there wasn't any more of the barrel left to scrape . . .'

I've named this one **Fred Thestair**.

Fred likes thinking he's bilingual because he can pronounce 'croissant' better than everyone else in Greggs and saying 'Worst theme park ever' when exiting Oak Furniture Land.

Review from the customer:
'Do I treat it with cream or just leave it alone and hope it goes away on its own?'

This one was requested by the lovely Ulrika, who asked if I could possibly use all my animal knowledge to draw this as a full-body portrait.

Not a problem at all, Ulrika. Not a problem at alllllll.

I don't know what he's called, but I've named him **Jarvis Socker**.

Review from the customer:
'I can't wait to get this off my hands . . .'

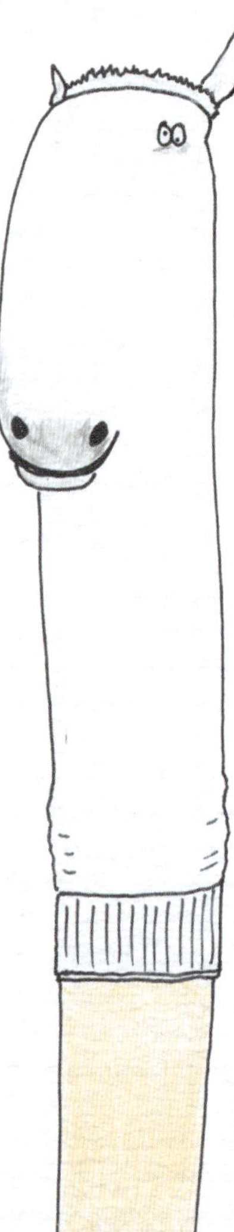

This free-range draught excluder belongs to the wonderfully lovely Fey Young. And if Fey's nickname isn't 'Egg' then she needs better mates . . .

I don't know what the cat is called, but I've named him **Clint Sleepsgood**.

Clint likes telling anyone who'll listen about the time he came fifth in the 2014 Welsh Snogging Championships.

Review from the customer:
'It looks like an anaemic dog turd going down a water slide . . .'

This portrait was requested by the wonderful Michael as a gift for his beautiful wife.

I don't know what she's called, but I've named her **Kath Ganhound** (the dog, not Michael's wife).

Review from the customer:
'Well, that's another thoughtless gift she's received from me. But at least this time the obvious lack of thought isn't from my side . . .'

I've named this pair of scamps **Immoral** and **Hardly**.

Stan and Oliver like selling guided trips to the end of the Sellotape roll, having an exaggerated appreciation of their daily water intake and attempting to break the Guinness World Record for the greatest number of S Club 7 lyrics tattooed on one forearm.

Review from the customer:
'It looks like a dishevelled sock-puppet leaning over an open toilet seat . . .'

I don't know what this lot are called, but I've named them **Snorty Spice**, **Starey Spice**, **Maybe Spice**, **Sloshed Spice**, **Union Jack Spice** and **Old Spice**.

Review from the customer:
'I'll tell ya what I want, what I really, really want . . .

A decent portrait of my guinea pigs.'

Folks, meet **Kevin Fart** and **Will Sniffed**.

Kev and Will like getting ideas above their station when practising parkour on National Rail property, calling the local bowling alley to see if they've got any strikes going spare and wearing double-denim swimwear whenever the opportunity arises.

Review from the customer:

'I don't know why you've sent me a picture of a couple of inebriated kangaroos, but can you let me know when the one of my dogs might be ready?'

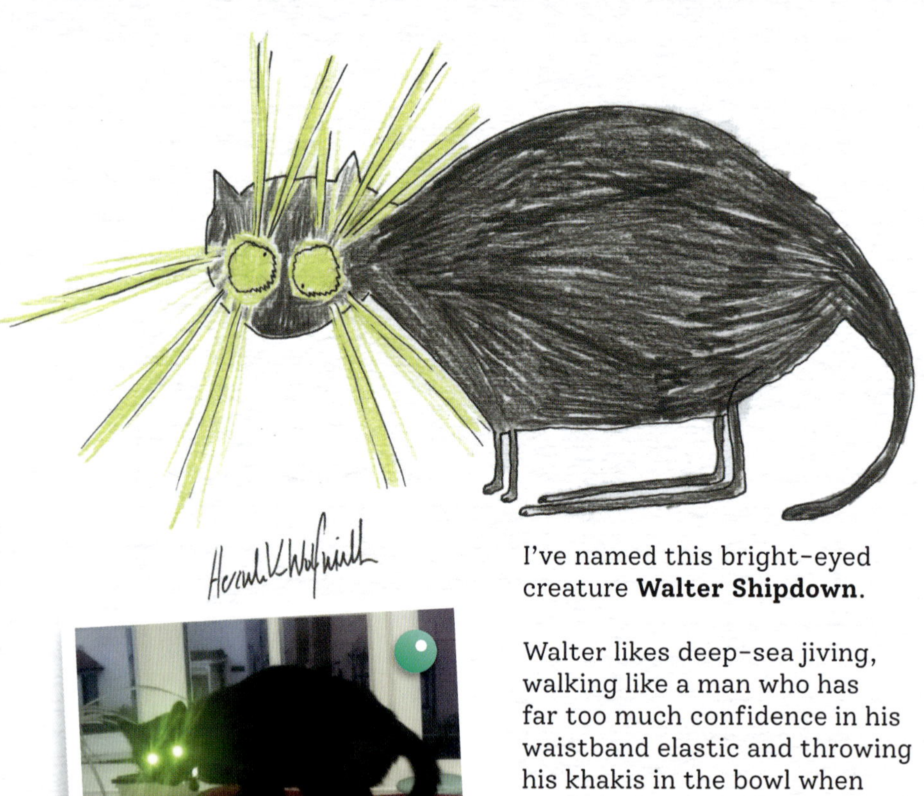

I've named this bright-eyed creature **Walter Shipdown**.

Walter likes deep-sea jiving, walking like a man who has far too much confidence in his waistband elastic and throwing his khakis in the bowl when attending his ex-military swingers' club.

Review from the customer:
'It looks like someone has thrown a couple of radioactive Brussels sprouts at a possum.'

I've named this dashing fella **Walter Kitty**.

Walter likes brushing past his secret crush on his street-cleaning rounds, and doing blow-offs that sound like a duck dealing with the conflicting emotions of a warm seat in a cold public toilet.

Review from the customer:
'Can you send me a digital copy, please? That should keep any viruses away from my computer.'

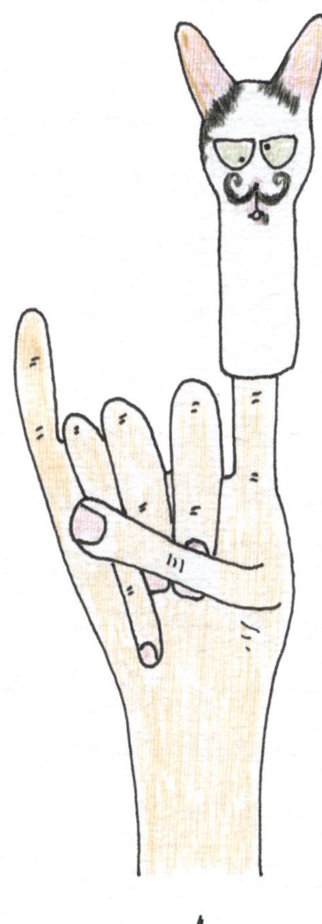

This beautiful pooch is called **Vicky Sawdust**.

Vicky likes slip-on self-consciousness, saying, 'Quick, hide your opinions,' whenever the father-in-law comes to visit and trawling the lonely-hearts adverts seeking someone to have a long-running argument with.

Review from the customer:
'I was hoping for something to put up, not something to put up with.'

This cute little Jack Russell is called **Alicia Squeees**.

Alicia likes saying, ‘I just want to get one thing straight . . .’ when starting an argument with her orthodontist and reporting her children to HR for harassment in the workplace when she’s working from home.

Review from the customer:
‘It’s a piece of art. Sorry, ART IN PIECES. It’s art in pieces. And in the bin.’

This old rocker is **Ozzy Waswarned**.

Ozzy likes telling people he once visited the Ferrero Rocher pyramid in Egypt, getting banned from church after multiple failed attempts at crowd surfing and saying, 'If I let you on here once, it's a slippery slope,' when working at the water park.

Review from the customer:
'It looks like a neglected set of bagpipes that have been abandoned at a rambunctious barbecue . . .'

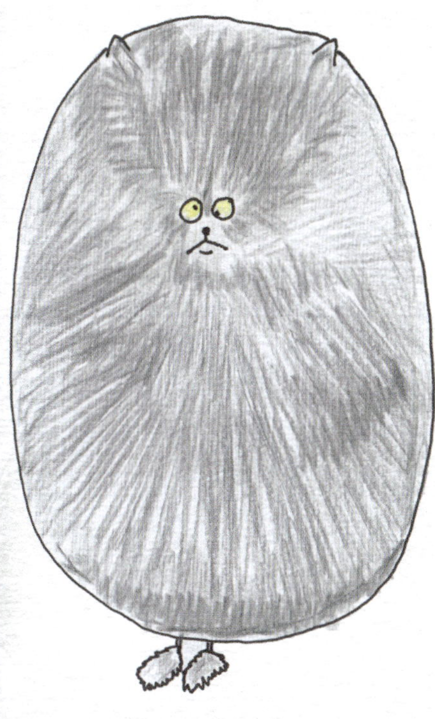

This could be an unusual variety of guinea pig, a baby owl or a close-up picture of Brian Blessed's chin for all I know, but I've named her **Hairy Magdalene**.

Review from the customer:
'You've captured in a few simple lines something that looks nothing like my cat. They're definitely a few simple lines, though.'

People are going to think I'm showing off with this one, but the reference photo submitted by the wonderful Kristen was just perfect in allowing me to show off my skills in capturing light and shadows.

I don't know what the pooch is called, but I've named him **Keanu Scuro**.

Review from the customer:
'They say that, on average, a person looks at a piece of art for eight seconds. I imagine your work brings that average down quite considerably . . .'

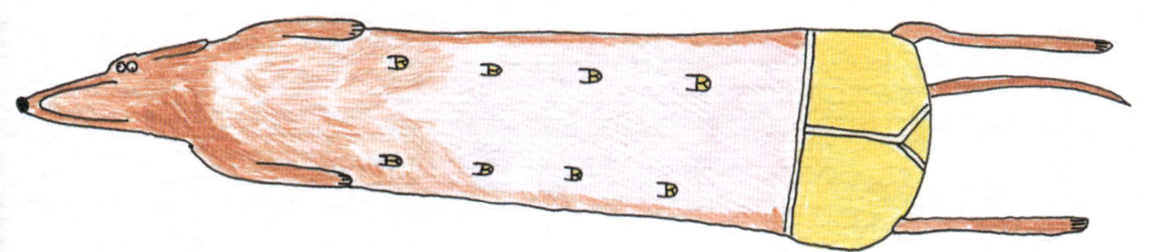

I've named this little cocktail sausage **Nora Bone**.

Nora likes involuntarily agreeing to her husband's requests every time the bus driver hits the brakes and saying, 'Serves four what? Hamsters?!' when reading the suggested serving numbers on a supermarket cake.

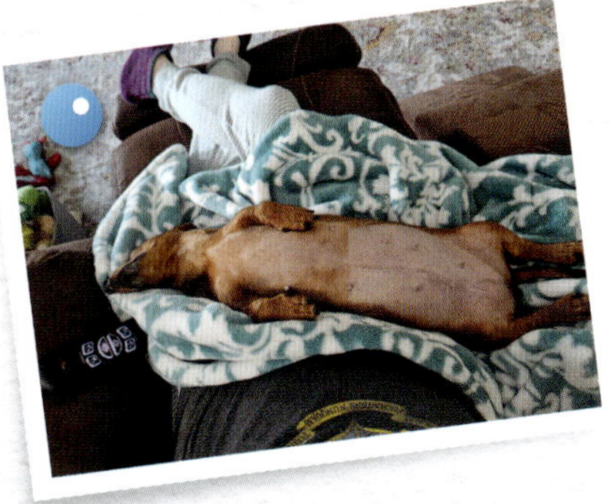

Review from the customer:
'I'd like to try to think of something positive to say . . . so I'm positive I don't like it!'

I've named this one **Alison Wonderland**.

Alison likes bitesize awkwardness, insisting to see the vicar's full service history when buying second-hand cake at the church fete and tirelessly lobbying the relevant authorities to have her backside officially declared an Ancient Monument.

Review from the customer:
'It's a journey through the senses. One that's left me feeling travel sick.'

I don't know what these boys are called, but I've named them **Neil Inclement** and **Chris Woe**.

Neil and Chris like going west, expressing their emotions through the medium of papier-mâché and saying, 'It's got three Michelin tyres,' when showing off about the quality of their local kebab van.

Review from the customer:
'What Have I Done to Deserve This?'

Picture credits

While every effort has been made to trace the owners of copyright material reproduced herein and secure permissions, the publishers would like to apologise for any omissions and will be pleased to incorporate missing acknowledgements in any future edition of this book.

p8 © Charlotte Harlen; p9 © Sarah Powell; p10 © Lou Atkinson; p11 (Cookie & Biscuit) © Emma Pugh; p12 © Aimee Aff Moore; p13 © Kathy Hodder; p14 (Himja) © Bessie & James Donnelly; p15 (Radley) © Kiah Hogan; p16 © Judith Dickinson; p17 © Caroline Fussey; p18 © Gina O'Shea; p19 © Shaun Harrison; p20 © Char Crooks; p21 (Lucy) © Sarah Dougherty; p22 (Shiner) © Christie Gwiner; p23 © Jayne Greenwood; p24 © Jess Thomas; p25 (Miss Marple) © Vickie Goodwin; p26 © Lucy Ann; p27 © Lo Victoria; p28 © Kate Cartmell Done; p29 © Lucy Sewill; p30 © Lillie Mae; p31 © Maura Quinlan Gordon; p32 © Lauren Carne; p33 (James) © Lisa Bolland; p34 (Pingu) © Carl Reynolds; p35 © Wladislaw Tschelnokow; p36 (Riley) © Nicole Phillips; p37 (Archie) © Amanda Carstairs; p38 © Jo Woodrow; p39 (Ras) © Vivian Fong; p40 © Maddie Smith; p41 (Lemmy) © Leanne Crosbie; p42 (Keda) © Laura Johnson; p43 (Fulga) © Vera Mayer; p44 (Monty) © Helen Walpole; p45 (Dottie) © Emma Szuster; p46 © Rachel Strong Wilson; p47 (Harry) © David Atkinson; p48 © Amy Weir; p49 (Maggie) © Trish Abbott; p50 © Liz Williams; p51 © Al Pal & Connie Eloise; p52 © Jody Tieking; p53 © Sharla Mazari; p54 (Holly) © Melanie Beighton; p55 © Zjena Lamour Jane Yerkovich; p56 (Hunter) © Nicola Smith; p57 (Zori) © Charlotte Davey; p58 (Quaver) © Georgia Tilbrook; p59 © Hayley Wainwright; p60 (Marvin) © Ruth Bennett; p61 © Eloise Marie; p62 (Sasha) © Alex Phillips; p63 © Emma Winfield; p64 © Kirstie Ireland; p65 (Boss) © Francesca Brown; p66 © Lucy Workman; p67 © Emma Pillow;

p68 © Joanna Kay; p69 (Phillip) © Kay Anderson; p70 © Summer Crabtree; p71 © Samantha Champion; p72 © Mio Chen; p73 © Claire Louise Davies; p74 (Smokey) © Claire Hanson; p75 © Paige Lawrence; p76 (Sega) © Jennifer Patricia Douglas; p77 (Arlo) © Charlotte 'Cozmo' Watkinson; p78 © Angie Hoskins; p79 (Timber) © Simon Stretton-Downes & Lucy Sellors-Duval; p80 (Wilma) © Jonathan & Stephanie Follebout; p81 © Ayeshea Rayner; p82 (Brahms & Missed) © Elsa Cooper; p83 (Baloo) © Arwen Makin; p84 © Laura Pennell; p85 (Stanley) © Amelia Maude; p86 (Gordon) © Lisa Hunt; p87 (Archie) © Jeannie Vaccaro; p88 (Snowy) © Jenny Dixon; p89 © Ian Peel; p90 © Lisa Stenning; p91 © Brenna Maus; p92 (Boo) © Georgia Alderson; p93 (Georgio) © Jessica Doran; p94 (Clemmie) © Tamsin Jordan; p95 © Nathaniel Campbell; p96 © Maria Olin; p97 (Balu) © Clare Green; p98 (Juno) © Claire Relf; p99 © Caroline Turner; p100 © Jo Patterson; p101 (Ralph) © Angharad Wilkinson; p102 (Nero) © Roslynne Bell; p103 © Hannah Bowman; p104 © Lauralyn Chrisley; p105 © Becky Warwick; p106 © Hannah DeRezza; p107 (Pippin & Gatsby) © Jennifer Walker; p108 © Teri Chadburn; p109 (Otis) © Joseph Williams & Kieran Robb; p110 © Ulrika Jonnson; p111 (Floki) © Fey Young; p112 © Michael Hyde; p113 © Deborah Carson; p114 © Katelyn Caldwell; p115 © Amanda Jane Price; p116 (Soppy) © Jo Hawley; p117 (Russell) © Emma Dawson; p118 © Danielle Adams; p119 © Melodie Bailey; p120 (Kiki) © Michelle Du Plessis; p121 (Disco) © Tanya Escobar; p122 (Vincent) © Kristen & Sean Mahaffey; p123 (Daisy) © Sara Abrams; p124 (Mikha) © Alise Polden; p125 © AC Hember.

HarperCollins*Publishers*
1 London Bridge Street
London SE1 9GF

www.harpercollins.co.uk

HarperCollins*Publishers*
Macken House, 39/40 Mayor Street Upper
Dublin 1, D01 C9W8, Ireland

First published by HarperCollins*Publishers* 2025

10 9 8 7 6 5 4 3 2 1

A catalogue record of this book is available from the British Library

ISBN 978-0-00-872069-8

Designed by Bobby Birchall, Bobby&Co

Printed and bound by PNB Print

MIX
Paper from
responsible sources
FSC™ C007454

This book is produced from independently certified FSC™ paper to ensure responsible forest management.

For more information visit:
www.harpercollins.co.uk/green

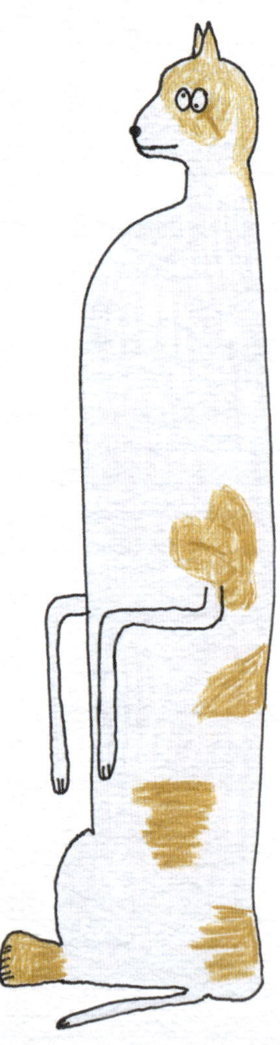